HASKELL W. HARR Drum Method

BOOK ONE

PREFACE

■ The purpose of this instruction book is to meet the needs of the young student aspiring to become a drummer in a school band or orchestra.

In writing this method, my aim has been to make it as nearly a self-instructor as possible. I have purposely omitted many of the drum rudiments, using only those that are necessary in playing the average drum part. Special emphasis has been given to the study of various time figures found in everyday playing.

In compiling the material in this method, I have acted on the suggestions of many bandmasters from all parts of the country as to subjects that would fit their particular needs, as well as using my own original ideas.

If the student will study seriously and try to understand this material, he can save not only some of his teacher's time, but will be able to eliminate unnecessary expense on his own part, through correct knowledge of the parts of his instrument, together with the proper manner of their assembly and care. ■

The Author,

Haskell W. Harr

To access audio, visit:
www.halleonard.com/mylibrary

Enter Code
7001-5391-7611-9356

ISBN: 978-1-4234-2026-2

7777 W. BLUEMOUND RD. P.O. BOX 13819 MILWAUKEE, WI 53213

Visit Hal Leonard Online at
www.halleonard.com

CONTENTS

INSTRUMENTS OF PERCUSSION

■ INSTRUMENTS of percussion are divided into two classes, those which produce a definite pitch when struck, and those which do not produce definite pitch. The tympani, bells, glockenspiel, celesta, and xylophone are included in the first class, while the snare-drum, bass-drum, tambourine, tom-tom, triangle, cymbals, castanets and gongs are in the second group.

Percussion instruments are also classed according to the materials used in their construction. The first, called the Autophonic group, are those in which the tone is produced by the vibration of solid bodies made of metal or wood. This group includes the bells, glockenspiel, gongs, celesta, xylophone, triangle, castanets, and cymbals.

The second, called the Membrane or drum group, are those in which tone is produced by striking a stretched membrane (drum-head). This group includes the kettle-drums (tympani), snare-drum, bass-drum, tambourine, and tom-toms. ■

THE DRUM

So far as is known, the drum was used early in the tribal history of every land in the world. The American Indians used drums to mark their time for their dances and to prophesy the weather, which was indicated by the change in the drum covering. The African Negroes danced to the beating of the tom-tom, and sent messages from tribe to tribe, by a drum code. Primitive people of today still use the drum for these purposes. The Egyptians, Assyrians, and Orientals had drums long before the days of written history, and archaeologists have found numerous examples proving them to have been beautifully designed and highly valued instruments.

With some exceptions, however, ancient peoples used the drum only to accentuate rhythm, but such drums as the kettledrums, or tympani, can be tuned, and are used, usually in pairs, to emphasize orchestral harmony. Kettledrums are large copper kettles, covered with vellum. The player controls their pitch by means of key screws which change the tension of the covering. Modern tympani also use pedals to allow a faster change of pitch.

On the other hand, the bass drum, the largest drum of all, gives out only a deep, indefinite tone. Its purpose is to mark rhythm. The snare or side drum is invariably associated with military bands, and the sound it produces is sharp and cutting. It is small, made of wood or metal, with a skin stretched across each end. Snares are stretched across one end and vibrate against the bottom head when the top head is struck. Another type, the tenor drum, is similar in appearance to the snare drum, but is larger and has no snares, and consequently its sound is not such a sharp one.

The sound produced also depends largely on the kind of drumstick used. Drumsticks may have wooden ends, leather covered ends, or ends of sponge or felt, thus varying the sound from a harsh, hard tone to a deep, smooth one.

THE SNARE DRUM

THE DRUMS used in the SCHOOL BANDS of today are classified as the DANCE drum, the CONCERT drum and the PARADE DRUM. The SIZES of these drums are as follows — the first number is the DEPTH OF SHELL, the second number is the HEAD DIAMETER.

DRUM SIZES

DANCE drum 5" x 14". CONCERT drum or ORCHESTRA drum 6½" x 14", 8" x 15". ELEMENTARY school PARADE drum 10" x 14". HIGH school PARADE drum 12" x 15".

THE PARTS OF THE SNARE DRUM

It is quite essential for the student to acquaint himself with all of the names of the parts of his instrument. The parts are listed according to catalogue names. Study the names of the parts, then find each part on the diagram.

Counter hoop
Batter head
Flesh hoop
Metal hoop snap eye
Internal tone control
Shell   Vent
Lug
Collar tension screw (rod)
Snare adjustment screw
Snare strainer
Snares   Snare bed
Snare gate.

COUNTER HOOP
BATTER HEAD
METAL HOOP
SNAP EYE
VENT
INTERNAL TONE CONTROL
ROD
SHELL
SNARE HEAD
FLESH HOOP
LUG
SNARES
SNARE
ADJUSTMENT SCREW
SNARE BED
SNARE GATE
SNARE STRAINER

On the inside of the shell are the re-inforcing hoops. These hoops should be made of thoroughly seasoned maple. Normal rings are ½-inch thick and 1-inch wide.

DRUMSTICKS

DRUMSTICKS are made in various lengths and weights, each designed to produce the BEST TONE on a SPECIFIC DRUM. "A" sticks are for the DANCE drum. "B" sticks for the CONCERT drum, "S" and "H" sticks for the PARADE drum.

The BEGINNING STUDENT should use sticks heavy enough to develop the WRIST MUSCLES and good CONTROL. The RECOMMENDED stick for elementary students is the "2B" (the "5A" for real small hands) and the "2S" or "1H" for high school students.

DRUMHEADS

DRUMHEADS are made of fine grain calf skins or plastic. The PLASTIC head is recommended for school band drums as they are not susceptible to changing weather conditions. When purchasing drumheads always specify if they are to be used for the BATTER side or the SNARE side, and if they are to be used for DANCE drums, CONCERT drums, or PARADE DRUMS.

THE CARE OF THE DRUMS

In order to obtain the utmost in performance, response, sound and durability of the percussion instruments, it is imperative that they are properly serviced and meticulously cared for. The following hints and directions should be adhered to in every respect if you expect your instruments to play well and to be properly preserved and neat in appearance.

TENSIONING DRUM HEADS

When tensioning drum heads, start with the batter head first, tighten clockwise around the drum.

1. Place key on tension rod, turn one-half turn to the right, and proceed around drum (keep finger on first rod as a marker).
2. Press forefinger on center of head. Proceed as above until there is very little "give" to finger pressure.
3. Loosen snares by turning knurled nut of snare strainer to the left.
4. Tap head about two inches from each rod with the drum stick. Head must sound the same at each rod. If not, make individual adjustment with the key.
5. Turn the drum over and adjust the snare head in the same manner.
6. The snare head must not be quite so tight so that it will vibrate against the snares.
7. Test in same manner as top head. Due to the two indentations on the shell called "snare beds", you will have difficulty getting the same pitch at the rods on either side of the snares.
8. After heads have been tensioned and the pitch evened up, tap the head with the drum stick and gradually turn the knurled nut of the strainer to the right until the snares come in contact with the head and give you a snappy, crisp tone of the well adjusted drum.

CARE OF THE DRUM

Drums should be taken apart and cleaned before the start of each school year.

It is important that all hardware be kept clean and dry. In the event percussion equipment is unavoidably exposed to inclement weather, all parts should be carefully and thoroughly wiped dry. Follow this with a cloth that has a small amount of light machine oil on it. This will prevent rusting.

Lubricate threads of tension rods with vaseline. Oil moving parts of the snare strainer and tone control with a light machine oil of the "2 in 1" type.

Maple and mahogany shells and hoops may be cleaned with water and mild soap. A damp rag will be an adequate scrubbing agent. Wipe dry. When thoroughly dry, apply a good furniture polish. Buff with a soft cloth.

Metal shells and hoops may be cleaned with a damp cloth, then wiped dry.

Pearl shells and hoops require less upkeep. To clean, wipe with a dry cloth.

Once you have the drum adjusted to a fine snappy tone, **do not loosen or tighten** the heads (skin) unless weather conditions require. In such a case, loosen the heads the same number of turns of the key when through playing, press the center of heads to take out the slack, and let dry.

PLASTIC HEADS

Apply plastic heads the same as skin heads. Apply a little more pressure the second day, and again the third day. The heads will then be set.

Dents will appear in a plastic head if tension is too loose, or if the sticks are too heavy.

When purchasing plastic heads be sure to mention whether they are to be used for parade drums, concert or dance.

SNARES

Snares should be adjusted so they are flexible enough to make a drum "speak" freely.

Wire Snares are the most responsive. Best used for dance band, concert band and orchestra.

Gut snares are best for parade and field drums where a heavy tone is required. Because they are affected by climatic conditions, snares on a drum so equipped should be kept tight when not in use. These snares are not recommended for indoor work where "p" and "pp" performance is required.

Be sure your snares strainer is in the "on" position when putting your drum away. Loose snares can easily get out of line.

RUDIMENTS OF MUSIC

A MUSICAL SOUND is called a TONE, and has four distinct properties; LENGTH, PITCH, POWER and QUALITY.

To indicate the length of tones, characters called notes are used. These NOTES bear specific relation to each other as indicated by their names. The student should study the chart below and MEMORIZE THE RELATION OF THESE NOTES TO EACH OTHER.

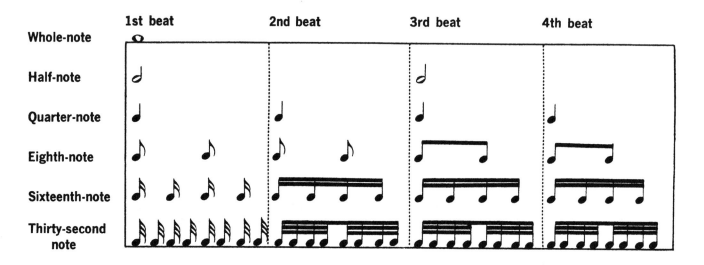

A DRUM BEAT loses its IDENTITY after a sixteenth note. GROUPS OF THIRTY-SECOND NOTES BECOME ROLLS AT A MARCH TEMPO.

TO INDICATE SILENCE, characters called RESTS are used, which bear the same relationship to each other as do notes. STUDY THE CHART BELOW.

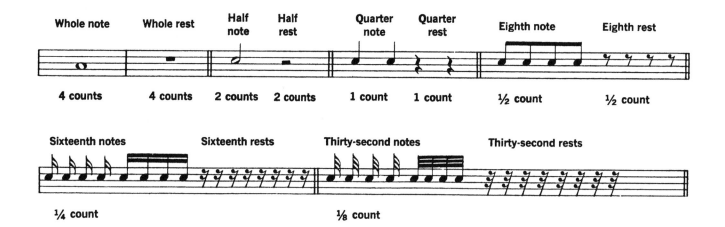

The PITCH of the tone is indicated by a character called the STAFF consisting of five parallel lines and their spaces, on which the notes are placed.

The staff

The staff with letter names of lines and spaces

6

HOLDING THE DRUM

FIGURE 1

FIGURE 2

Figure one shows the CORRECT WAY to carry the PARADE DRUM. The sling rests on the RIGHT SHOULDER and passes **diagonally across the body** and hooks together at the left hip. Adjust the sling so that the TOP HOOP of the drum is approximately THREE INCHES BELOW THE WAIST, just far enough to have a **slight bend in the right elbow when playing.** The drum should rest directly in FRONT OF THE LEFT LEG. A leg rest, fastened to the drum just to the right of the snare strainer, will assist in controlling the drum when marching.

Figure two shows the position of the CONCERT DRUM on a stand. It should be the same height and angle as when carried on a sling.

BUTT   SHOULDER   BEAD

HOLDING THE DRUMSTICKS

In order to develop TECHNIQUE, CONTROL, and the proper ATTACK and RELEASE, it is necessary for the student to have the correct method of holding his drumsticks. There are many ways of holding drumsticks, depending on the style of drumming being done. The beginner should start with the traditional method, as taught in this book.

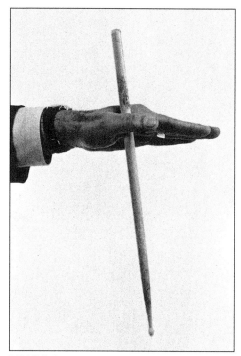

FIGURE 1

THE LEFT HAND

Extend the left arm, palm of the hand down, fingers together, as shown in the picture at the left. Place the stick in the SOCKET between the THUMB and FIRST finger, with one-third of the stick (from the butt end) above the hand. The grip should be just tight enough to cause a slight drag if you try to pull the stick from the hand. Study figure 1.

Close the third and fourth fingers and TURN THE ARM TO THE LEFT. The stick will then fall into position **across** the **third finger,** as shown in figure 2.

Draw the arm towards the body, allow the first and second fingers to CURL TOWARDS THE STICK to act as a guide for the stick, and you will have the closed hand position for playing as shown in figure 3.

Your hand should now be in the following position: Stick BETWEEN thumb and first finger, FIRST TWO FINGERS lightly against the stick, THIRD FINGER CLOSED and acting as a **support** for the stick, FOURTH FINGER resting against the third. **The thumb is always above the stick.**

FIGURE 2

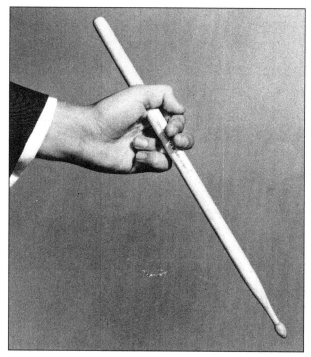

FIGURE 3

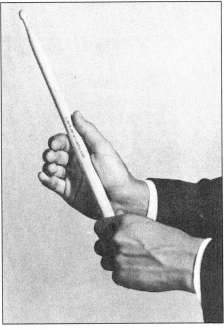

FIGURE 1

HOLDING THE RIGHT STICK

Place the stick DIAGONALLY across the PALM of the hand. Grip between the FIRST FINGER and the THUMB one third of the distance from the butt end of the stick. Figure 1.

Close the fingers LOOSELY around the stick. The SECOND FINGER will be used to **help control the stick.** Figure 2.

TURN THE HAND OVER, so that the BACK of the hand will be up when playing. The stick will be approximately in a straight line with the wrist and arm. Figure 3.

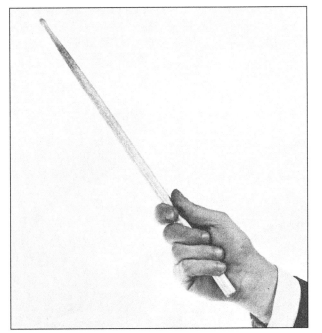

FIGURE 2

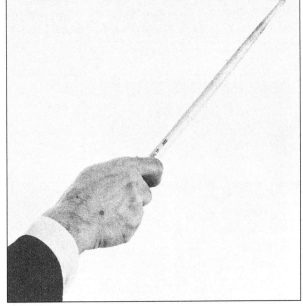

FIGURE 3

THE LIKE-HAND HOLD

In this manner of playing the left stick is held the same as the right stick. This is not a new hold, it has been used by professional drummers for years. There is no particular advantage in playing this way, although I would advise all students to learn this method. When playing on the rim, wood blocks, bells, et cetera, the effect is better holding the sticks in the same manner.

Learn the traditional stick hold first, as shown in this book. You will have no difficulty in changing the left hand stick hold. The student starting with the like-hand hold does have difficulty changing to the traditional hold when required to do so.

The photographs on this page are used to illustrate the most common errors in holding the stick and making strokes.

FIGURE 1.

Held between end of thumb and first finger. Not in socket between thumb and first finger. See figure 2, page 8 for correct way.

FIGURE 2.

Stick held to tight bead "jabbed" into head. Apt to break the head. See figure 2. page 11, for correct way.

FIGURE 3.

Arm and hand moved straight up and down, with no wrist movement. See figure 2, page 11, for correct movement.

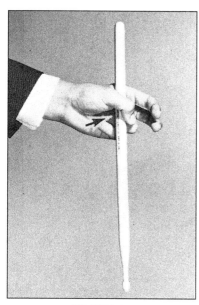

FIGURE 4.

Stick held too tight, by bending thumb over stick. No bounce to stick. See figure 2, page 8, for correct way.

FIGURE 5.

Stick held between second and third fingers, palm up. See figure 2, page 8, for correct way.

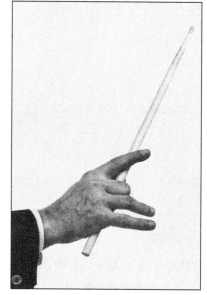

FIGURE 6.

Stick held with fingers sticking out. Hand too rigid. See figure 2, page 8, for correct way.

LESSON FOUR

MAKING THE STROKE

POSITION: Stand erect (all practicing should be done while standing), have the drum in a position so that the head will be about five inches below the waist.

THE RIGHT STICK

Place the bead of the stick on the head, slightly off center. Raise the arm until the hand is on a level with the chin, at the same time turn the wrist outward, causing the bead to travel in a half-circle. See dotted line in figure 1.

TO COMPLETE THE STROKE, return the stick to the head with a motion similar to **cracking a whip.**

Be sure that the drum is low enough to allow the arm to hang nearly straight down.

Practice the following exercise until each of the notes can be struck evenly with the same amount of force. See that they are spaced evenly. Take your time, be sure that the stroke is made correctly.

R — Right stick

FIGURE 1

R R R R R R R R R R R R R R R R R R R R R

THE LEFT STICK

Place the bead of the stick on the head. Raise the arm until the hand is on a level with the chin, at the same time turning the wrist outward. To complete the stroke return the stick to the head with a motion similar to **flipping water from the fingers.**

Be sure that the wrist is turned out as the arm is raised. Many make the mistake of raising the arm straight up and down without turning the wrist. The stick must be free.

Another common error is to hold the stick tightly across the third finger knuckles with the thumb. To avoid this, have the thumb touch the first joint of the first finger.

Practice this exercise the same as the one above.

L — Left stick

FIGURE 2

L L L L L L L L L L L L L L L L L L L L L

ALTERNATING THE STICKS

OFF CENTER CONCERT DRUM

CENTER PARADE DRUM

In the previous lesson we studied how to play with each stick individually. We will now start to use both hands, one after the other, called ALTERNATING.

Draw a circle on the head, or pad, about two inches in diameter, in the CENTER OF THE DRUM. The object of the circle is to keep the sticks as close together as possible when playing.

The pitch of the drumhead varies. The tone in the center of the head is dead, due to the strain applied by the tension rods pulling from all sides. The farther away from the center you play the higher the pitch of the tone.

If you would play with one stick near the center of the drum and the other stick about half way between the center and the hoop, you would have two different pitches and the playing would sound uneven.

By playing with each stick an equal distance from the center of the head you will have an even tone. Study the diagram at the left.

Check the sticks to see that they are of the same weight. This may be done by striking them on a hard surface. If they are the same, the pitch of each stick will sound the same when struck.

Study the exercise below, pay particular attention to the sticking, notice that at first you have four beats with each hand, then three, then two and then one. Use the same amount of force for each blow, space the notes evenly. Count out loud.

R R R R   L L L L   R R R R   L L L L

R R R L L L R R R L L L R R R L L L

DOUBLE BAR
(End of strain or piece)

R R L L R R L L R L R L R L R L R L

COUNTING TIME

It is very important to have a method of "COUNTING TIME" to develop and maintain a **perfect sense of rhythm.**

A good musician DOES NOT use a VISIBLE means to BEAT TIME, but to the beginner any mechanical means that will aid in gaining musical expresson, especially in counting time is advisable. Of the different methods used, I believe the use of the foot and the voice to be the best for the drummer.

In using the foot to beat time, raise it from the floor slightly, then lower it and raise it again. Thus ↓ down ↑ up. When the foot touches the floor the beat starts. To complete the beat the foot must raise and come down again.

The use of the voice allows even greater division of notes than the foot. In a measure of 4/4 time count 1-2-3-4, one beat for each quarter ncte. To divide the quarter note into eighth notes and count them, add the word "and" after each number, thus: 1 and (&) 2 & 3 & 4 &. The quarter notes may be divided into sixteenth notes and easily counted by adding the letter "E" after the 1, and the syllable "Ah" after the AND, thus 1 e & ah, 2 e & ah, 3 e & ah, 4 e & ah.

LESSON SIX

In order that we may be able to play together, and in time, TIME SIGNATURES are used. They are placed at the beginning of a piece of music, AFTER the CLEF SIGN.

TIME SIGNATURE: The TOP number tells us that there are four beats in every measure. The BOTTOM figure tells us that the quarter note gets one beat.

FOUR-FOUR time is called COMMON TIME and is then indicated by the letter C used in place of the figures 4/4.

Two dots placed before a double bar :‖ are called a **REPEAT SIGN.** DEFINITION: when you reach a REPEAT SIGN go back to the FIRST DOUBLE BAR; If no DOUBLE BAR go back to the BEGINNING.

SUBJECTS: 4/4 time. A QUARTER NOTE gets **ONE** beat, a QUARTER REST **ONE** BEAT.

R — right hand   L — Left hand

🔊② MEMORIZE THE ABOVE TIME FIGURES, **then play the study written below.** The exercise is written as a drum part from an easy beginners band book would be written. The lower notes are for bass drum.

Bass drum, sometimes marked B. D.

LESSON SEVEN

INTRODUCING EIGHTH NOTES

THE EIGHTH NOTE ♪ TWO EIGHTH NOTES equal ONE QUARTER NOTE in time value. To simplify reading, whenever two or more eighth notes are written together, **the stems are connected by a solid line** ♫ or ♫♫ . To play the eighth notes in the first exercise, DIVIDE THE BEAT by adding the word AND after each number, thus: 1 & 2 &
1 & 2 &

MEMORIZE the above time figures, then try the exercise written below to apply them. COUNT OUT LOUD.

14

LESSON EIGHT

QUARTER NOTES ♩ QUARTER REST 𝄽 — EIGHTH NOTES ♪♪ or ♫

Continuation of time figures using eighth notes, quarter notes and quarter rests.

LESSON NINE

INTRODUCING THE EIGHTH REST

Quarter note ♩ quarter rest 𝄽 — Eighth note ♪ EIGHTH REST ⁊

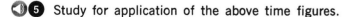 Study for application of the above time figures.

16

LESSON TEN

Continuation of time figures using eighth notes, ♪, and eighth rests, 𝄾
Stand erect while practicing. Count out loud.

1 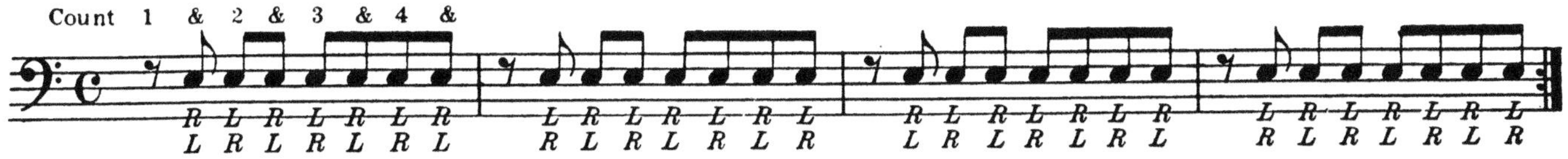

2 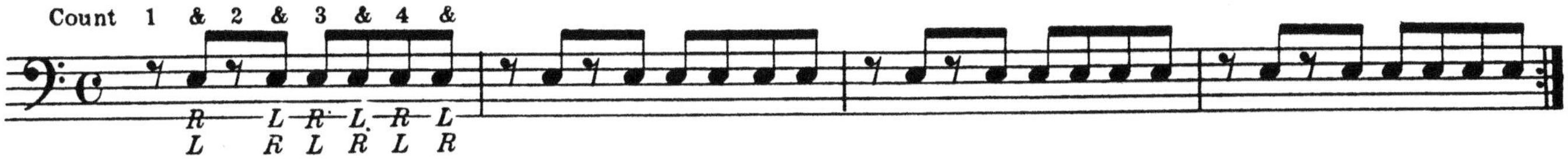

3 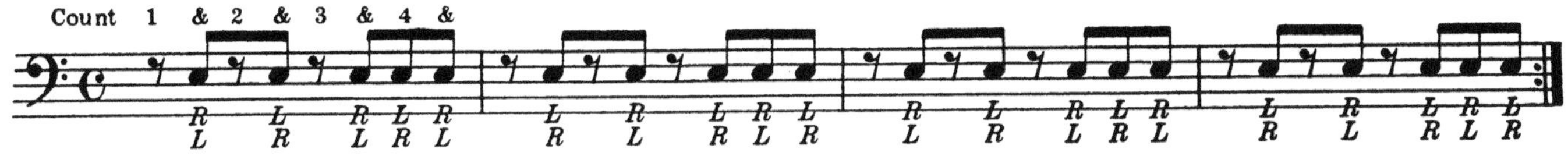

4 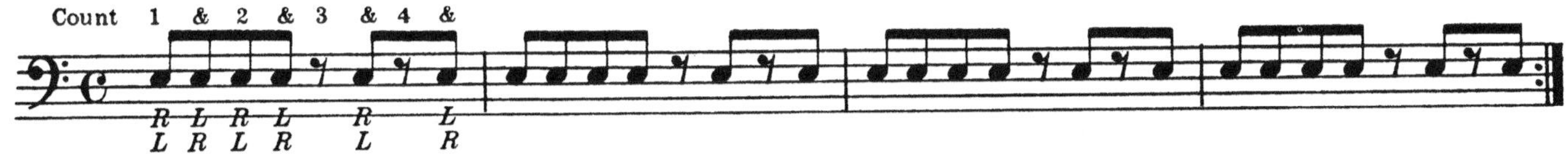

5 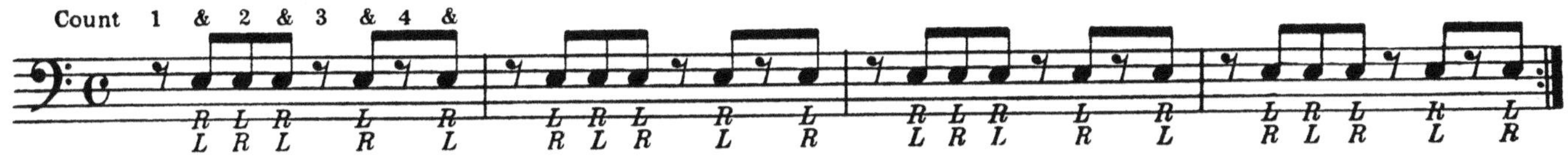

6 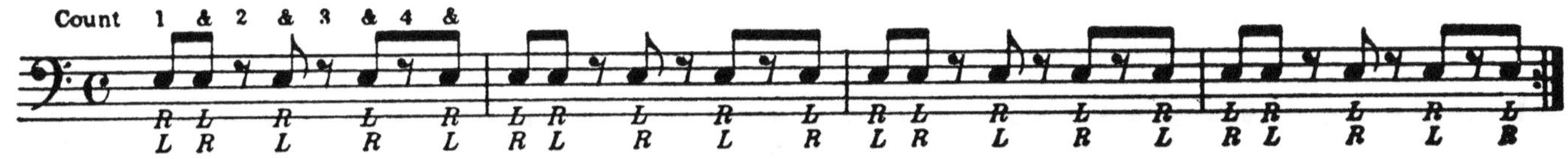

7 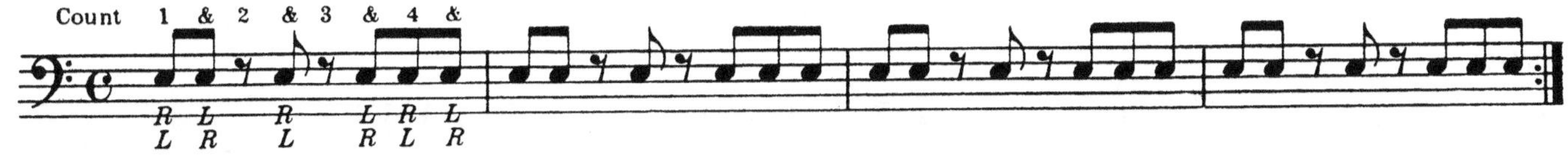

8 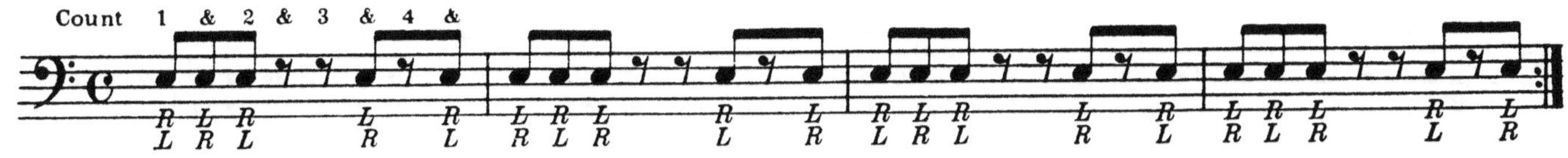

6 Study for the application of above time figures.

9 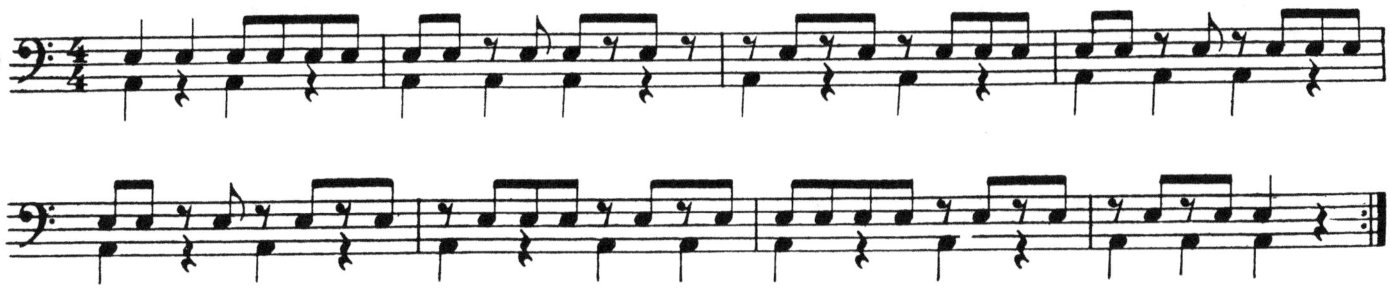

LESSON ELEVEN

Application of previous time figures as written in drum parts of band music. The NEW SUBJECTS included in this lesson are; EXPRESSION MARKS and ENDINGS.

Forte	(𝆑)	loud—strong
Fortissimo	(𝆑𝆑)	louder than *Forte*
Piano	(𝆏)	softly
Pianissimo	(𝆏𝆏)	softer than *Piano*
Crescendo	(◁)	gradually louder
Diminuendo	(▷)	gradually softer

FIRST and SECOND ENDINGS

Play the first ending, then repeat. The second time skip the first ending and play the second.

* 🔊 **7** Watch carefully for the expression marks and endings. 🔊 **8**

* From this point on, listen to the drum part on the recording, then play along with the accompaniment track on the repeats.

LESSON TWELVE

NEW SUBJECT D.S. al Fine.

D.S. is the abbreviation for DAL SEGNO (däl-san'-yo) from the sign.

𝄋 is the sign most frequently used where there is a D.S.

FINE (fe'-ne) **the end.** Whenever you find the term **D.S. al Fine,** you will **go back to the sign** and play until you reach the word Fine.

NEW —— FERMATA ⌢ means hold, if placed over a note; the end if placed over a double bar.

Moderato – in moderate time.

LESSON THIRTEEN

SUBJECTS: WHOLE REST ▬ 4 counts

HALF REST ▬ 2 counts.

EXPRESSION MARKS.

REPEAT MEASURES

REPEAT SIGNS. ‖: :‖

ENDINGS. ┌1 ┐ ┌2 ┐

20

SUBJECT: 2/4 TIME   In the previous lessons we have had four beats, or counts in each measure. In this lesson we start with TWO BEATS in EACH MEASURE, a QUARTER NOTE getting ONE BEAT AS BEFORE. **Play the quarter notes heavier than the eighth notes.**

Exercise for application of above time figures. **Pat the foot on the bass drum notes.**

LESSON FIFTEEN

REVIEW — 2/4 time — 2 counts to each measure.
A quarter note gets one count.

Play **quarter notes heavier** than **eighth notes.**

Expression marks — *p*—soft; *mf*—moderately loud
f—loud; *ff*—very loud

First and Second endings

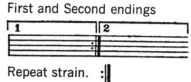

Repeat strain. :‖

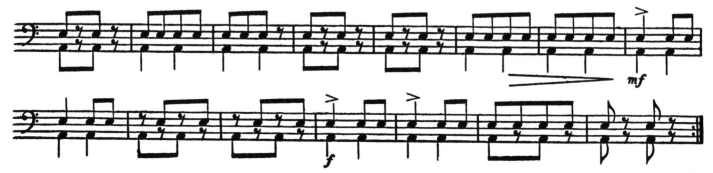

22

LESSON SIXTEEN

NEW SUBJECT. SIXTEENTH NOTES, written or . Two sixteenth notes equal one eighth note in time value.

COUNT EIGHTH NOTES 1 & 2 &   COUNT SIXTEENTH NOTES 1 e & ah 2 e & ah.

NOTE: Play eighth notes louder than sixteenth notes.

The following study may be used for a street march for drums.

LESSON SEVENTEEN

SUBJECT: Continuation of time figures using eighth notes, sixteenth notes, and eighth rests.

Exercise may be used as a street beat.

LESSON EIGHTEEN

SIXTEENTH NOTES ♪   SIXTEENTH RESTS ⅞

The SIXTEENTH REST has the same time value as the SIXTEENTH NOTE. It is written with TWO flags on the stem.

Exercise may be used as a street beat.

LESSON NINETEEN

Continuation of time figures using sixteenth notes, and sixteenth rests.

Exercise for application of above time figures.

LESSON TWENTY

New Time figures using sixteenth notes and sixteenth rests.

Exercise

SUBJECTS: Expression marks or dynamics.

DOUBLE REPEAT MEASURES. | ⨪ | Whenever the REPEAT MARK is written through TWO MEASURES the TWO PREVIOUS MEASURES are to be played again.

Follow carefully ALL MARKS OF EXPRESSION. COUNT OUT LOUD. **Watch repeats and endings.**

LESSON TWENTY-THREE

RHYTHM is a large part of ALL music and there are very few people who can not learn how to apply it. The student must learn the FUNDAMENTALS OF RHYTHM. When marching with a band you must feel the pulsation and rhythm of the music to enable you to "KEEP IN STEP" with the music. The TIME SIGNATURE determines the **rhythmical pattern of the beats within the measures.** This PATTERN is made up of STRONG and WEAK beats which occur and recur in regular and definite succession, **when the notes are equal in time value.** The stronger of the beats occur on the first count of each measure. When a composer desires a certain note or group of notes to have more emphasis than the others, he usually indicates the notes by placing an accent mark (>) above them.

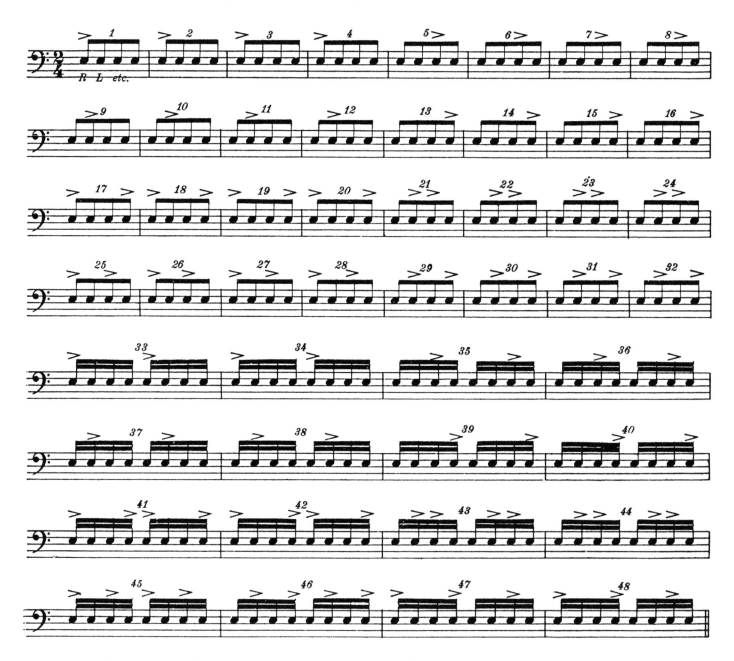

Play the following exercise in march tempo, pay strict attention to the accents.

30

In the previous lessons we have studied notes of short time values. We will now study a method of sustaining notes of a longer duration.

This method of sustaining the notes is done by playing a series of short notes, rapidly alternating the hands. AS EACH STICK STRIKES THE DRUMHEAD it is allowed to REBOUND ONCE, **then stopped** (see lesson 24). **These hand movements and rebounds make the roll.**

Only the rolls most commonly used in the band books adapted for the use of grade and high school students will be studied in this book. The tempo of the roll will be 120 beats per minute. The BASIC NOTE of the roll is the 32ND NOTE (♪). For clarification I will call each time the stick touches the drum a STROKE. Example: Two eighth notes tied together, with three lines through the stem of the first note, designate a roll (♫). The first eighth note contains four 32nd notes, stroke, bounce, stroke, bounce (four taps), the second eighth note will receive a single tap. This is called a FIVE STROKE ROLL.

To encourage the young drummer in playing in the band, I will suggest the following system for the student who may be able to play his time figures quite well, yet is unable to develop a good roll. Divide the notes designated as rolls into sixteenth notes and play with single strokes. In this manner he will have the correct number of hand movements learned when he is capable of bouncing the sticks and playing his roll as it should be played.

A **TIE** is a curved line ‿ connecting two notes on the same line or space. In drumming, the second note is always played with a single tap.

THE MULTIPLE STROKE or BUZZ ROLL

The student should always learn the stroke and rebound rudimental roll first. This will develop wrist and muscle control. The multiple stroke roll is used in concert playing where more finesse is desired.

THE MULTIPLE STROKE ROLL. Raise the tips of the sticks as high as possible using the WRISTS ONLY. Upon making the stroke, allow the stick to bounce freely two or more times.

The sticks must bounce not less than two inches, each stroke being brought down with equal force.

Try to allow the stick to bounce until the next stick strikes. The last note of the roll is a single tap, and must not bounce.

For EVENNESS OF ROLL, **each stick must strike the head the same number of times.**

CARBON PAPER TEST

Place a piece of carbon paper on the drumhead, carbon side up. Cover with a piece of writing paper. Have the student play the roll on the paper. Turn the paper over and check the number of marks made by each stick.

THE CONTROLLED REBOUND of the LEFT STICK. Make the stroke with the same snap used in playing the single strokes. Immediately after the stick contacts the head, apply pressure with the thumb by rolling it slightly to the right, thereby forcing the stick back to the head for the second blow. At the same time turn the wrist outward, allowing the third finger to pick up the stick as before.

Left hand study.

The CONTROLLED REBOUND of the RIGHT STICK. Immediately after the stick has rebounced from the first blow, apply pressure towards the bead of the stick by bearing down lightly with the knuckle of the index finger, forcing the stick back to the head. When the stick hits the head the second time tighten the grip with the second finger and snap the wrist outward as before.

Right hand study.

As soon as the student has mastered the rebound, he should start alternating the hands, using single strokes at first to enable him to have smooth arm and wrist movement, then bounce each stick to form the Long Roll.

THE FIVE STROKE ROLL

The FIVE STROKE ROLL is played "HAND TO HAND". It has THREE PRIMARY STROKES, or hand movements, the first two movements are bounced, the **third hand movement is always played with a single stroke.** When played in series it is played right, left, right,-then-left, right, left. It may have an accent at the beginning, or at the end, depending on whether the roll starts or stops on the beat. **Practice both ways.**

ANALYSIS:

Play the following exercise with single strokes, then repeat and bound the strokes on each sixteenth note. Notes in the ties will develop into the Five Stroke Roll.

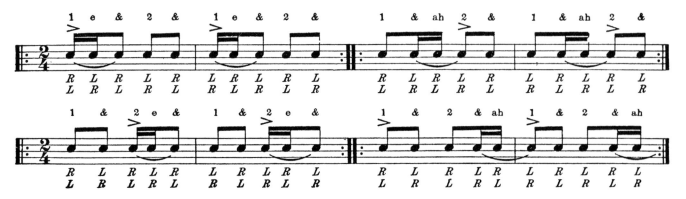

LESSON TWENTY-FIVE

Study for FIVE STROKE ROLLS   Carefully observe all marks of expression.

THE SEVEN STROKE ROLL

The SEVEN STROKE ROLL is not played from HAND TO HAND. It usually starts with the left hand and ends with the right. This roll is designated in two ways, first by a quarter note (𝄽) and second by the same notation as the FIVE STROKE, two eighth notes tied together. Practice this roll with an ACCENT on the FIRST TAP for use when the roll STARTS ON THE BEAT, and then with an ACCENT on the LAST TAP when it ENDS ON A BEAT.

Play the following exercise with SINGLE STROKES until you have the feel of the hand movements, then repeat and BOUNCE THE STICKS on EACH SIXTEENTH NOTE. WATCH THE ACCENTS.

THE NINE STROKE ROLL

The NINE STROKE ROLL is played from HAND TO HAND, the same as the five stroke. The roll has FIVE PRIMARY STROKES. The first four are BOUNCED and the fifth is SINGLE. The roll is designated by a QUARTER note tied to an EIGHTH note. Practice this roll by applying the accent to the FIRST beat, then again with the accent on the LAST beat.

Play the following exercise with single stroke first time, bounce the sticks on the sixteenth notes the second time.

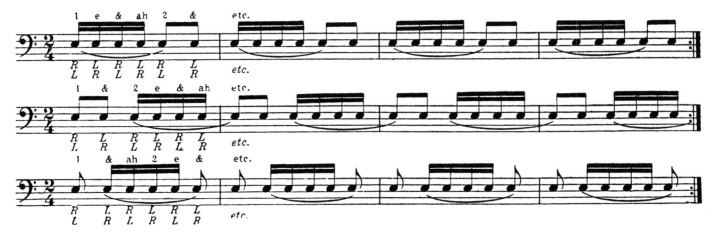

LESSON TWENTY-SEVEN

THIRTEEN STROKE ROLL

The THIRTEEN STROKE ROLL is played **hand to hand,** the same as the five and the nine, the accent being on the last stroke. It is seldom used where the accent would be on the first beat, but it is well to practice it both ways.

SEVENTEEN STROKE ROLL

The SEVENTEEN STROKE ROLL is played from **hand to hand,** although it is never written in series. There are **nine hand movements,** the **first eight** are **bounced,** the **last stroke single.**

Study for the Five, Nine, Thirteen and Seventeen stroke rolls. Watch carefullly for the accents.

LESSON TWENTY-EIGHT

SUBJECTS:

FIVE STROKE ROLLS SEVENTEEN STROKE ROLLS   NINE STROKE ROLLS

Carefully observe all marks of expression. **Play the accented notes heavier.**

Start all nine stroke rolls in this exercise with the right stick. Alternate the five stroke rolls.

36

LESSON TWENTY-NINE

SUBJECTS: FIVE STROKE ROLLS   THIRTEEN STROKE ROLLS

SEVEN STROKE ROLLS   SEVENTEEN STROKE ROLLS

*The correct roll for this figure is the seven stroke roll. As it is customary to separate heavily accented notes in band work, I recommend the five stroke roll be used in its place.

**To play this measure count it 1-+-2-trip-i-let. Bounce the sticks on trip-i-let for six of the notes of the roll.

Review all exercises and substitute the MULTIPLE STROKE ROLL, page 31.

LESSON THIRTY

NEW SUBJECT:

When 4/4 time is played at a rapid tempo, the number of beats per measure is changed from 4 to 2, and the time is called "Cut time" or "Alla Breve". A HALF NOTE now receives ONE beat instead of a quarter note.

The "**C**" which stood for "COMMON TIME" is now cut in half by a line "**¢**" to denote two beats instead of four.

Sometimes 2/2 is used instead. 2/2 signifies that the HALF NOTE receives one beat, and there are 2 beats in a measure.

When playing the following exercise, pat the foot **down** on the note designated for the Bass drum and **up** on the following rest, counting 1 & 2 &.

LESSON THIRTY-ONE

TIME FIGURES in ALLA BREVE or CUT TIME. Notice that a measure of eighth notes in cut time is counted the same as a measure of sixteenth notes in 2/4 time.

A whole note o in ¢ time = 2 beats.

A half note ♩ in ¢ time = 1 beat.

A quarter note ♩ in ¢ time = ½ beat.

An eighth note ♪ in ¢ time = ¼ beat.

Study for application of above time figures.

LESSON THIRTY-TWO

SUBJECT: CUT TIME. ROLLS IN CUT TIME.

Five stroke roll 2/4 time   Five stroke roll Cut time

Nine stroke roll 2/4 time   Nine stroke roll Cut time

Seventeen stroke roll 2/4 time   Seventeen stroke roll Cut time

TRIO

LESSON THIRTY-THREE

SUBJECT: CUT TIME. ROLLS.

Five stroke rolls . Nine stroke rolls . Seventeen stroke rolls .

Pat the foot on the bass drum note.

TRIO

LESSON THIRTY-FOUR

TRIPLETS

A TRIPLET is a group of THREE notes having the same time value to that amount which the group displaces. For example: A group of three eighth notes may replace one quarter note ( ) or two eighth notes ( ) in which case the three notes would be played in the one beat of the note or notes it replaced. The TRIPLET is usually designated by the figure 3 written either above or below the group. The TRIPLET is one of the most difficult time figures to play smoothly. Much time must be spent in its study.

Common errors in playing. Right way , Wrong way or or .

42

LESSON THIRTY-FIVE

DOTTED NOTES

A dot (.) placed after a note adds ONE-HALF of the value of the note itself. Thus a dotted half note (𝅗𝅥.) is equal to THREE QUARTER NOTES (♩♩♩) in time value. The half note was equal to two quarter notes and the dot, adding one half of the value of the note, added one more quarter note to its value. A dotted quarter note (♩.) is equal to three eighth notes (♫♪). A dotted eight note (♪.) is equal to three sixteenth notes (♬♬).

43

THE FLAM

THE FLAM plays such an important part in drumming, that it is well to thoroughly understand it before attempting to play it. It is a combination of a STROKE and a TAP. The difference between the stroke and tap is as follows. A stroke is made with an arm and wrist movement, while the tap is made with the wrist alone. It is written by placing a small note (grace note) before a large note (♪♩). Beats containing FLAMS should not be attempted until the FLAM is mastered, otherwise the effect will be lost.

The purpose of the FLAM is to broaden the sound of the tone. The sticks do NOT strike the head at the same time, but they must strike so close together that it will sound as one stroke.

The Flam gets its name from the hand that plays the principal note. There are three flams, the right flam, left flam, and the alternate flams. Alternate flams are played from hand to hand, the hand that plays the stroke of the first flam stays close to the drum to be in position to play the grace note of the second flam. This develops a swinging motion from side to side. Many students develop the swinging motion and yet strike the same stick first each time, usually the right, instead of reversing the position.

Two rudiments commonly used in 6/8 time are the FLAM ACCENTS NOS. 1 & 2. They will be studied in this section of the book. Many composers do not understand the rudiments of drumming, therefore their application is left mostly to the discretion of the performer and the director. To help in the interpretation of the parts I will give a few examples of the method I use in determining when and when not to use the flams.

It will be necessary for the drummer and the director to study the parts carefully and bear in mind that we are attempting to have the drum parts fit in with the parts as played by other instruments of the band. Also keep in mind that the purpose of the flam is to broaden the tone.

Flam accent No. 2   Flam accent No. 1

The quarter notes in measures 1 and 2 are played heavier and are sustained by the wind instruments. To get the desired effect on the drum it will be necessary to flam the quarter notes. Measures 3 and 4 are played lighter and smoother. I would play the drum part as written. Measures 5 and 6, being heavily accented would require the flam on the accented beats.

LESSON THIRTY-SEVEN

RIGHT HAND FLAM (Parade)

Start with the right hand at chin level, stick pointing straight up, the left stick with the bead two inches above the center of the drum or pad. Tap the two inch beat very lightly and return the stick to two inches above the drumhead. Almost simultaneously with the tap, strike a solid blow with the right stick, and the instant the stick strikes the head squeeze it with the fingers tight enough to prevent it from bounding up. When the left stick strikes the head say FA, when the right stick strikes the head say LAM. When the control improves the Fa-Lam closes to Flam, which is just as the beat should sound.

RIGHT HAND FLAM (Concert)

Start with the bead of the stick about six inches above the drumhead, arm nearly straight down, left stick in the same position as above. Just after the left stick strikes the head, make a heavy blow with the right stick and stop the same as above.

Practice the exercise below for the development of the flam. Keep the right hand high while playing the grace notes. After playing the fourth grace note with the left hand make the stroke with the right hand.

LEFT HAND FLAM (Parade)

Start with the left hand at chin level, stick pointing straight up, the bead of the right stick about two inches above the drumhead. Play a light tap with the right hand. This tap is followed immediately by a heavy left stroke. The right stick is returned to the two inch position. The left stick is stopped at the two inch position by applying pressure with the thumb, which holds the stick solid between the thumb and the ring finger.

LEFT HAND FLAM (Concert)

Start with the left forearm parallel with the floor, turn the wrist back as far as possible, bead of the stick should be at least six inches above the drumhead. The right stick in the same position as above. Make the heavy stroke with the left hand with the same motion as when shaking water from the fingers. The heavy left stroke follows immediately after the tap with the right stick. Use the exercise above for practice.

WHEN PLAYING FLAMS one stick should always be higher than the other.

Keep the left hand high while playing the four taps with the right hand. After the fourth tap make the stroke with the left hand.

ALTERNATE FLAMS

The first flam is started with the right hand at chin level, stick pointed straight up. The left hand is held down with the bead of the stick about two inches above the drumhead. Make a light tap with the left stick and immediately raise the hand to chin level. The tap of the left hand is followed immediately with the heavy blow of the right stick. As soon as the right stick strikes the head, apply pressure with the fingers and stop the stick two inches above the head. You are now in position to play a left flam, which is played in reverse. The right stick now plays the light tap, which is followed by the heavy left stroke.

The sticks are stopped in the same manner as explained on the previous page.

If the main stroke is played with the right hand it is called a RIGHT FLAM, if with the left it is a LEFT FLAM.

As the speed increases, the hand which plays the heavy stroke is gradually brought closer and closer to the drumhead.

In concert music when flams appear in rapid succession it is often possible to play them more smoothly if they are all played the same way.

FLAM ACCENT NO. 1

Flam Accent No. 1 is used in 6/8 time marches, and is composed of a flam and two taps, usually written in pairs.

L R L R R L R L

Start with the right stick about six or eight inches above the drum or pad, bead of the left stick two inches above the pad. Play a right flam, raising the left stick three inches above the drum. Stop the rebound of the right stick three inches above the drum. Make a left tap and raise the bead of the stick to six inches above the drum. Make a right tap and return the stick to the same level. You are now in position to start the next flam. Play the next flam accent in reverse. To play this rudiment say—Flam-left-right-flam-right-left.

L R L R R L R L L R L R R L R L L R

⊕ = Raise stick

FLAM ACCENT NO. 2

Flam Accent No. 2 is also used in 6/8 marches. Start with a right flam. Immediately after playing the left tap of the flam, raise the left stick to about six inches above the drum. After striking the heavy blow with the right stick, stop the rebound about three inches above the drum and play the next tap from that position. Return the stick to about two inches above the head. You are now in position to play the next flam. Play the next movement in reverse. Notice that the flam and the tap are separated by an eighth note. Always play this rudiment with the sticking shown.

L R R R L L L R R R L L L R

SUBJECT: 6/8 TIME. The TOP FIGURE tells you there will be six counts in each measure, the LOWER FIGURE 8 tells you that an eighth note will receive one beat. A quarter note will receive two counts, a dotted quarter note three counts and a dotted half note six counts. Watch the sticking carefully. Use the same pattern through the playing of 6/8 time.

When playing a March written in 6/8 time, we count 1,2,3,4,5,6, in each measure, but beat or step two steps to the measure. The first three eighth notes are included in the first count, the 4th, 5th, 6th in the second beat. To simplify counting, count: *1 & ah 2 & ah*
1 2 3 4 5 6

It is sometimes necessary to abbreviate notes to save space. A quarter note with a line through the stem (♪) is to be played as two eighth (♫) notes. A dot after a note adds one half of its value, thus a dotted quarter note with a line through the stem (♪.) will be played as three eighth (♫) notes. These three notes will be played on one beat in 6/8 time.

Street beat

*NOTE: Dots represent number of notes to be played

LESSON FORTY

RHYTHM ROLLS IN 6/8 TIME

The tempo governs the number of strokes of a roll. In 6/8 March time you play a greater number of notes per beat, than in 2/4 time, therefore you will play fewer strokes for a roll in 6/8 time than you would the same notation in 2/4 time. Example: 2/4 thirteen strokes   6/8 7 strokes.

The basic note of the roll in 6/8 march tempo (120 beats per minute) is the 16th note. When playing the **measured roll,** the **8th note** is bounced. In exercise one, the dotted half note roll has six eighth notes, five of which are bounced, the sixth played with a single tap. This is an eleven stroke roll.

If the roll is too open, and more finesse is desired, substitute the multiple stroke roll, but use the same hand movements.

Start all rolls beginning on the first count with the right stick in 6/8 time. Start those beginning on the second count (fourth eighth note) with the left stick.

There has always been considerable controversy as to which is the correct roll to play for the following time figure. Some recommend the five stroke roll, others the seven stroke. However, it will take an exceptionally good drummer to play even the five stroke roll and not take up any more time value than is allotted to the figure. To the student, I would recommend the five. Play the roll slightly faster.

Street beat

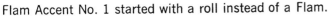

Flam Accent No. 1 started with a roll instead of a Flam.

TIME FIGURES IN 6/8 TIME

NOTE: SEVEN STROKE ROLLS in 6/8 tempo are played by starting with the right hand as well as the left hand. Play rolls open first, then substitute the multiple stroke rolls. Keep the hands moving in rhythm.

Street beat

LESSON FORTY-TWO

ADDITIONAL TIME FIGURES IN 6/8 TIME

Notice that the two sixteenth notes in exercise are both played with the same stick. This is done in order to keep the same rhythmic pattern of Right hand on the first eighth note and the left hand on the fourth eighth note (second beat in march tempo). Play multiple stroke rolls on slow tempos.

LESSON FORTY-THREE

ADDITIONAL STUDIES IN 6/8 TIME

Five stroke rolls ♪.   Thirteen stroke rolls ♪♪   Seven stroke rolls ♪♪

Play Flams on the quarter notes.

Stop all dotted quarter note rolls on the dot.

*The numbers placed over the measures are to assist in counting the measures to be repeated.

LESSON FORTY-FOUR

SUBJECTS: APPLICATION OF FLAM ACCENTS NO. 1 & 2.

Study the lesson carefully before starting to play. Be sure that you understand all the rudiments contained in the lesson. Watch all marks of expression. Play Flams on the quarter notes.

*Count measures two & three—1-2-3-4-5-6&. Play the five stroke roll by bouncing the stick on- 6&, and playing a single stroke on the one of the next measure.

52

SUBJECTS: FLAM ACCENT NO. 1.   FLAM ACCENT NO. 2.   ROLLS.   FLAMS.

LESSON FORTY-SIX

SUBJECT: THE RUFF.

The RUFF is composed of two grace notes and a principal note 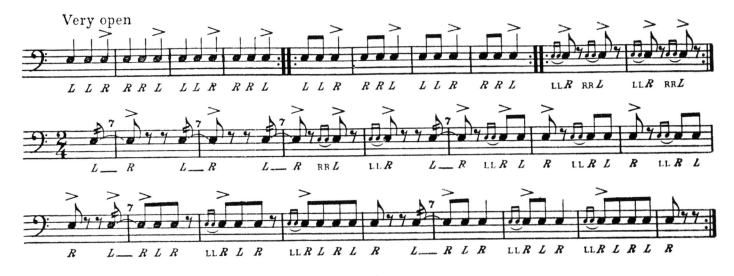. It is played with the same hand motion as the FLAM. One hand starts high, one low, and **both** start down at the same time, one striking just ahead of the other. The beginner should observe that there is the distance between the first and second grace note that there is between the second grace note and the principal beat. Upon striking the drumhead the low hand makes a bounce (like the bounce when playing a roll) which is followed immediately by the main stroke. The sticks, when they hit the head sound 1-2-3, not 1-2--3. Count 1-2-3 rest, 1-2-3 rest, etc.

LLR   LLR

When playing the ruffs, the principal note is struck exactly on the beat. The time allotted for the grace notes is taken from the preceding note.

THE FOUR STROKE RUFF

The FOUR STROKE RUFF is composed of four notes, three grace notes and the principal note. It is very effective if properly executed. The three small notes are played lightly and the fourth note is accented. It is used extensively in numbers of the patrol nature. It is played with single strokes, generally from left to right, L R L R.

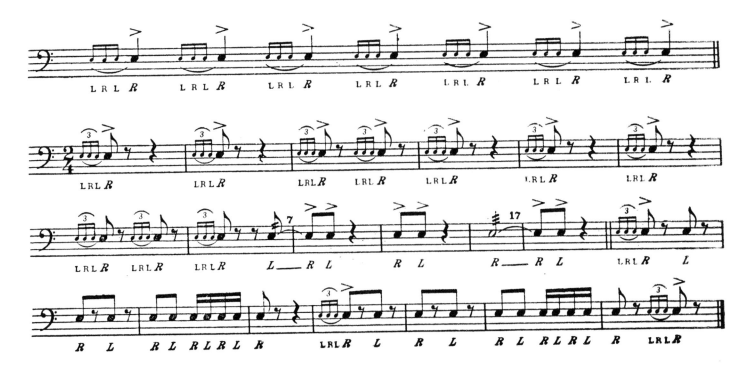

LESSON FORTY-SEVEN

THREE-FOUR TIME

So far we have had lessons in 4/4, 2/4, 6/8 and ¢ time. The following lesson is in 3/4 time. You are to count three beats in each measure, giving a quarter note one beat, a half note two beats, a dotted half note three beats, etc. Be careful in counting the time. 3/4 time is often referred to as waltz time.

* Length of roll governed by speed of exercise

LESSON FORTY-EIGHT

SUBJECT: CONTINUATION OF EXERCISES IN 3/4 TIME. Watch carefully the division of the count and beat, then practice to acquire evenness.

SYNCOPATION

SYNCOPATION occurs when the usual accent in a bar is displaced, and results from tying notes in an unaccented part to those in an accented part; or from weak accent to strong accent, also from placing long notes between shorter ones. **An accent should always be given to the syncopated notes.** The mark over or under the note is the "accent sign."

LESSON FIFTY

To those who have trouble with the time, divide exercises 1&2 into eighths, counting 1&2&. Divide the other exercises into sixteenths, counting 1-e-&-a 2-e-&-a. The accent should be distinct, but not too strong. Just enough to make the note stand out a trifle, and to help keep the rhythm steady. Syncopation is a forced accent on the part or parts of the bar.

THE BASS DRUM

The bass drum is the largest member of the drum family. Although it does not have any definite pitch, it is one of the most important instruments of the band. The principal object of the bass drum in any musical organization is to hold an even rhythm and to help with the phrasings and accents.

There are many fine points in the art of playing bass drum, they will require much thought, study and observance, and plenty of good common sense. A poor bass drummer can do more towards breaking up the rhythm of an organization than any other man.

ANTICIPATING THE BEAT

The performer selected to play the bass drum should be one with a good sense of rhythm. He must be always on the alert for any change of tempos of his leader. He must study his director, as well as his music, to be able to anticipate the beat. He must remember that the tone of his drum is deep and travels much slower than the instruments of higher pitch. His position being in the rear of the band will call for him to strike the drum just ahead of the beat in order for the tone of the drum to travel to the rest of the band, otherwise he will be accused of "dragging his beat." That one point must be given much serious thought. It is much easier for the director, to have you crowd the beat a little than it is to have you "drag."

THE SIZE OF THE BASS DRUM

The size of the bass drum to be used will depend greatly on the size of the organization, and, if it is to be used for parade, on the size of the boy who will be required to carry it.

I would suggest a drum 14 inches deep and 28 or 30 inches in diameter for a band up to about forty pieces, and one about 16x36 inches for larger bands. For parade use a 10x28 inch Scotch bass drum.

The depth of a drum should not be over one-half of the diameter of the head. To increase the volume of a drum, increase the head diameter. To increase the depth would give more of a muffled tone.

THE BASS DRUM BEATER

For concert playing the soft lamb's wool beater will give a deeper and more musical tone. The beater should have a large ball on one end and a smaller one on the other end. This will allow the drummer to play a roll on the drum with one hand. For parade work a hard felt stick gives the sharper tone one prefers.

THE BEATING SPOT

Playing in the center of the drum produces a dull thud, as you play more towards the rim the tone becomes higher in pitch and more resonant. Each drummer will pick his own beating spot, depending on the tone desired and the size of the drum. The most common beating spot is about halfway beween the center and the rim.

THE CARE OF THE BASS DRUM

Because of the size of a Bass Drum many drummers pay little or no attention to its care. The heads of the bass drum are just as important as those of the small snare drum. Care should be taken that the heads are of the same thickness, especially on drums that do not have separate tension tightening rods. The batter head should be the tighter of the two to allow for the loss in air transmission of the blow from the batter head to the oppsite head.

If the heads are not of the same thickness on the single tension drums, by that I mean drums that have both heads tightened by the same rod, the strong spot on one side will pull a weaker spot on the opposite side down farther and cause the drum to become lop-sided.

Tension the heads the same all around, test the tone of the head at each rod and get the same pitch at each post.

BASS DRUM (Cont'd)

MUSICAL NOTATIONS

The top notes in a drum score are written for the snare drum, the lower ones for the bass drum and cymbals. Unless otherwise indicated the cymbals are played with the bass drum at all times. When the composer desires the bass drum to be played alone it is commonly marked "B.D." or "B.D. only." It is then played alone until marked "Tog." (together) or, "B.D. and cymbals." A cymbal solo is often indicated by a diamond shaped note ⟨ ♩ ⟩, or with the abbreviation "Cym." over a regular note. Example:

In playing notes of different time values on the bass drum; such as whole notes, half notes, quarter notes, etc., we follow the traditional method of the wind instruments, namely, the largest note in the measure receives the most volume. In other words, a half note would be struck harder than the quarter note next to it.

POSITION

The bass drummer should stand in any organization, so that he may be able to watch the director at all times. Place the drum on a stand high enough to allow him to stand erect while playing the instrument. Place the music stand in a position where it will be in a direct line between the player and the leader.

The bass drummer should also play the cymbals in concert work, as he is better able to balance the tone of both. It is very difficult to get two players to keep the bass drum and the cymbals together and at the same time keep the tonal balance required. A separate cymbal player should be used to get special accented cymbal beats where a certain effect is desired.

The lower cymbal should be fastened to the drum shell by a good holder, of which there are many styles.

The upper cymbal should be held with a strap. Never use a wooden handle. The solid handle clamps to the cymbal and has a tendency to muffle the tone. The leather strap allows freedom of tone and also permits the use of many flash cymbal movements which increases the showmanship of the drummer.

THE CYMBAL KNOT

Push the four ends of the strap through the hole in the cup of the cymbal. Lay the four ends flat on the cymbal and number them, 1-2-3-4, (fig. 1). Fold number 1 to the right over number 2 (fig. 2). Fold No. 2 downward over No. 1 (fig. 3). Fold No. 3 to the left over No. 2 (fig. 4). Fold No. 4 upward over No. 3 and under No. 1 (fig. 5). Pull the ends tight and you have a knot that will not loosen (fig. 6).

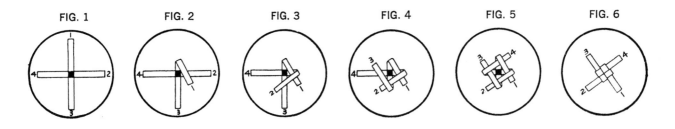

FIG. 1   FIG. 2   FIG. 3   FIG. 4   FIG. 5   FIG. 6

BASS DRUM (Cont'd)

THE STROKE

Make a full arm downward swing, twist the wrist to the right and strike the head a glancing blow with an upstroke. This will produce a much better tone than when striking the drum on the downward movement.

To complete the movement raise the stick to a level with the head, back of hand up. Many flash movements of the stick may be worked out with this style of stroking that will add much color to your work. One beat commonly used is the figure 8. Much time will be required to play the flash beats in tempo, but it is worth the effort.

The photograph at the left shows an arm stroke that should be avoided. It is a straight-to-the-head movement a beginner is apt to try, which results in a slow, sluggish arm movement and does not produce a good, snappy tone.

Always remember that a bass drum should be struck with a glancing blow.

CYMBALS

The tone of the bass drum should not be muffled by allowing the beater to remain against the head.

To silence the tone of the drum for staccato notes, or to stop the ringing tone at the end of a strain, roll the fingers of the right hand against the head, 5-4-3. See the photograph to the right. Be careful not to allow the beater to strike the head when you roll the fingers against it or it will sound like you have played an extra note.

Many bands are now using a tone control for the bass drum to help in silencing the ring of the drum, the tone control being fastened to the side of the drum opposite the batter head.

PLAYING THE CYMBALS

Heavy cymbals are the best for band work, the size of the cymbals depending on the size of the boy who is to play them. Fourteen or fifteen inch cymbals are about the best size for all around playing and will not be too heavy for the average boy to play. Have one cymbal securely fastened to the drum hoop. The leather strap makes the best holder for the top cymbal, as it allows the tone to ring out.

To get the best tone strike the cymbals together with a sideward motion, bringing the top cymbal away quickly.

Cymbals struck squarely together with an up and down motion form a vacuum and the tone is muffled. The effect when the cymbals are "clamped" together is similar to the tone of the foot pedal cymbal used by the dance drummer for after beats. It is very effective when used by the bass drummer on the after beats when playing popular music.

CYMBAL SOLOS

To play a cymbal solo, hold the cymbal overhead and with full arm movement strike the cymbal with a downward blow of the bass drum beater. Strike near the edge.

For a flashy effect, give the wrist a little twist to the left as you strike the cymbal and you will be able to spin it in a complete circle.

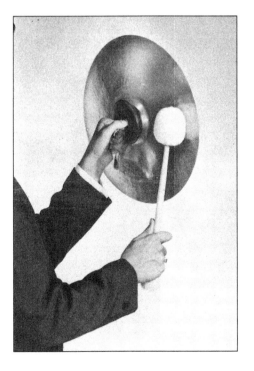

CYMBALS (Cont'd)

For special cymbal solos and for street playing the individual cymbal player uses two cymbals that he holds by flexible leather straps. Cymbal pads cushion the blow to his hands.

The cymbals are brought together with a glancing up and down blow in the form of an ''arc.'' (See illustration.)

For sustained loud cymbal notes raise the arms high in the air after striking.

To silence the cymbals the individual cymbal player presses them against his body to stop the vibration at the end of the piece, or for staccato notes.

The concert bass drummer who plays cymbals and bass drum together stops the vibration of his cymbals by flexing the wrist so that the top cymbal will come in contact with his coat sleeve, while the lower cymbal is muffled by bringing his forearm or coat sleeve against it.

THE USE OF TRAPS

The use of traps in descriptive selections is very essential to build up the desired effects. The proper way to play the different traps should also be studied by the drummer. I will give a few suggestions on the use of the three main effects, namely, the triangle, the castanets, and the tambourine.

THE TRIANGLE

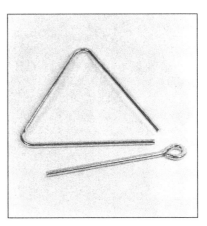

The triangle part is very important. The triangle should be suspended at a convenient place where it can be played by either drummer. It may be suspended from the music stand by any one of the handy holders on sale, or by just a piece of cotton cord. Use a medium sized triangle as close to A in pitch as possible. Suspend with the open side to the left. Use a metal beater, NEVER use a drumstick. To produce the roll, hold the beater lightly in the left hand and move the beater rapidly back and forth across the corners. To silence the tone, touch lightly with the hand.

THE CASTANETS

Castanets are used in the playing of music of the Spanish style. They are made of ebony or black walnut. The dancer uses castanets in pairs, large and small, that are held in the palm of the hand and are clicked by the fingers. The drummer will find it more convenient to use the ones mounted on a center piece of hard wood, with handle attached. See photograph. For sharp staccato notes, strike the castanets against the drumsticks held loosely in the left hand. To produce the roll, hold the castanets by the handle and shake rapidly.

THE TAMBOURINE

A light tambourine should be selected, with a large number of jingles. Hold firmly with the left hand and tap with the thumb and fingers about an inch and a half from the rim to get the best results. To produce the ruffs and short rolls, wet the thumb and rub it along the edge. Long rolls and notes that are held are made by shaking the tambourine. To produce the accented notes strike with the right hand. A very good "pp" can be made by resting the tambourine on the knee and gently tapping it with the fingers of the right hand. Tambourines are used mostly in Spanish music.

Handle your tambourine carefully and do not let the jingles rattle, as this will give the audience a hint that you are about to play it. Half of the effect of small traps is lost when it does not contain the element of surprise.

Look out for your castanets, and be careful that you do not bang your triangle beater down on the stand so hard that it can be heard above the playing. Such sounds, although unconsciously made, are heard by the audience as distinctly as are other sounds made by the drummer, and are positively as bad as if the part were played incorrectly. These are little things, but it is the little things that count. There are a thousand and one details that must be remembered and cared for before your work will show the schooling and finish necessary to distinguish yourself as a first-class drummer.